TEACH YOURSELF TO PLAY

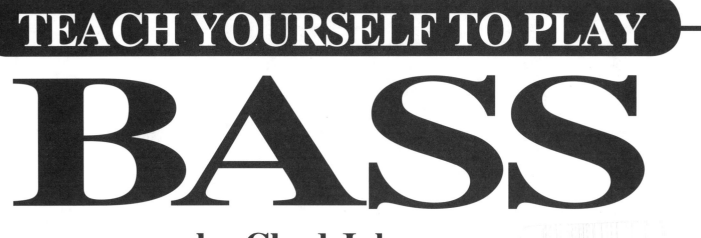

BASS

by Chad Johnson

T0061425

This is the place to learn the bass!

In this book, you'll learn a fast and effective method for playing the bass guitar. Get started immediately and learn at your own pace while in the comfort of your home.

To access audio visit:
www.halleonard.com/mylibrary
Enter Code
3625-2861-7707-8227

ISBN 978-1-4950-2619-5

HAL•LEONARD®
CORPORATION

7777 W. BLUEMOUND RD. P.O. BOX 13819 MILWAUKEE, WI 53213

In Australia Contact:
Hal Leonard Australia Pty. Ltd.
4 Lentara Court
Cheltenham, Victoria, 3192 Australia
Email: ausadmin@halleonard.com.au

Visit Hal Leonard Online at
www.halleonard.com

Introduction

So you've decided to learn the bass guitar. Excellent choice! You've also chosen the perfect learning tool—this book—to begin your musical journey. You don't need to be able to read music, nor do you require any musical experience, to use this book. *Teach Yourself to Play Bass* makes use of tablature, combined with rhythmic symbols, which makes for a quick and pain-free learning curve. The bottom line is that you can start right now!

We'll begin this book by looking at the parts of the bass, the bass amplifier, and the techniques used in both hands. Posture is also important, so don't skip this part! We'll continue with an explanation of the tablature system, rhythm notation, and fretboard diagrams. After that, we'll plunge into the examples, which will begin with open strings and gently progress in difficulty throughout the book. Topics along the way will include chord symbols, scales (major and minor), octaves, 5ths, arpeggios, and more. Each section will feature examples (performed on the accompanying audio tracks) that span several musical styles, so you'll be developing your versatility right from the start!

The objective here is to get you playing the bass as quickly as possible but also put you in a position to continue learning and improving once you've completed the book. By working through the examples, you'll not only be improving your technical skill on the instrument, but you'll be assimilating a myriad of musical concepts without even knowing it, including common chord progressions, rhythms, and melodic and formal structures. These overarching topics will be applicable to every instrument—not just the bass—and will therefore increase your musical ability as a whole.

While we want you to start playing bass right away, it's important that you develop good habits from the beginning. Therefore, be sure to thoroughly read (and re-read, if necessary) all instructions before diving into a set of examples. When you reach the end of a chapter, quickly review it before beginning the next one to make sure you're in good shape to tackle the new material. Regarding your practice sessions, you'll make much more headway if you practice for shorter periods of time more frequently than if you cram one six-hour session into every Saturday. Of course, you have to work with what you have available; however, as is often the case, you can find an extra 30 minutes a day if it's important to you. Remember to have fun with it!

Table of Contents

Chapter 1
Getting Started

Parts of the Bass

Before you put your hands all over it, you should probably get acquainted with a bass guitar first (at least take it out to dinner!). The image below details the most common features found on electric bass guitars. Each model will likely be slightly different, but they'll usually have most, if not all, of these features in common.

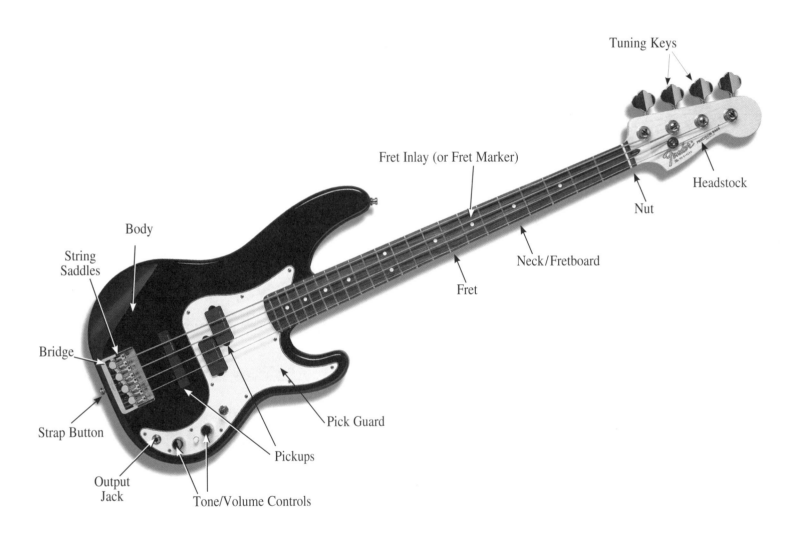

Your bass may have more than one pickup, it may not have a pick guard, or it may have more or fewer volume/tone controls. If that's that case, don't sweat it—just be sure to familiarize yourself with the features of *your* bass.

Fretboard Diagrams

Let's look closer at the neck of your bass. Those metal strips that run across it—perpendicular to the strings—are called *frets*. Frets help us produce different, distinct pitches on each string and are numbered, low to high, from fret 1 to fret 20 (or 21 or 22, depending on your bass), with fret 1 being closest to the nut.

We sometimes use fretboard diagrams to depict portions of the neck for the purpose of showing certain notes, scales, etc. You may see these oriented vertically or horizontally, although horizontally is more common for the bass (vertical diagrams are used more often for guitar chords). See below for a description of how they work.

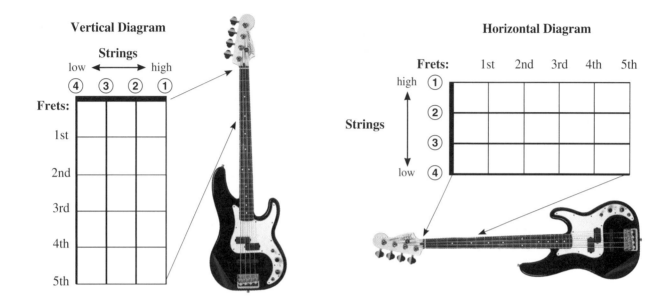

Vertical Diagram

The vertical diagram is like looking at the instrument hanging on a wall. The vertical lines represent the strings, with string 4 (the thickest, lowest pitched) located far left. The horizontal lines represent the frets, with the lowest fret number (often the nut) at the top. Again, though these are more common for guitar, you may see them for bass occasionally.

Horizontal Diagram

The horizontal diagram is the more commonly used fretboard diagram for bass and the one we'll use in this book. This diagram is closer to a player's perspective. It's oriented as if you'd laid the instrument across your lap. The horizontal lines represent the strings, with string 4 (the thickest, lowest pitched) located at the bottom (or nearest your midsection). The vertical lines represent the frets, with the lowest fret number (often the nut) at the left.

Fret-hand Fingers

For simplicity, the fretting hand may be referred to as the "left hand" in this book, and the plucking hand may be referred to as the "right hand." If you're a leftie, just reverse these labels whenever you see them. The fingers of the fret hand are numbered as follows:

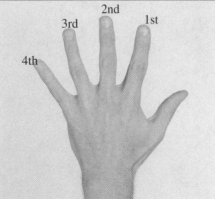

String Pitches

As mentioned earlier, the strings of the bass are referred to, with regard to high and low, by their music pitches—not their geography. This is a bit confusing at first, and you will certainly hear some people calling string 4 the "high" string because it's the highest from the floor. However, string 4 is actually called the "low" string because it produces the lowest pitch. When tuned correctly, each string of the bass sounds a specific pitch. From lowest to highest, they are as follows:

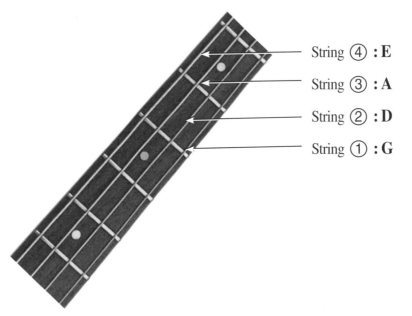

String ④ : **E**

String ③ : **A**

String ② : **D**

String ① : **G**

Of course, if you've ever seen a bass player play, you know that they don't just play open strings. We use the frets to play different notes, as well. The lower the fret number (toward the nut), the lower the pitch; the higher the fret number (toward the bridge), the higher the pitch. We'll discuss this in more detail soon enough.

Left-Hand Technique

In order to produce clean, accurate playing, you need to be mindful of the proper playing techniques for the instrument. Bad technique can not only lead to "sloppy" playing; in the worst cases, it can even lead to injury. Take this section seriously!

See the photos below for proper left-hand technique.

Place your thumb on the middle or underside of the bass neck.

Place your finger just behind the fretwire in order to produce the cleanest-sounding note.

Don't let your palm touch the neck of the bass.

Also remember these important fretting tips:

- Only use as much pressure as necessary. Pushing down too hard can cause the note to go sharp (too high) and lead to finger fatigue.

- If you place your finger too close to the fret or too far back (in the middle of two frets), you could get a buzzing sound. The cleanest tone is produced with your finger directly behind the fret.

Right-Hand Technique

There are two common methods used for plucking strings on a bass: with the fingers or with the pick, or *plectrum*.

Playing with the Fingers

This is the most common method of playing bass and is used in virtually all styles—from jazz and country to the heaviest of metal. To begin, rest your thumb on the pickup and place your index finger on string 4. Using the pad of the finger (not the tip), and keeping the knuckle closest to the tip straight, push slightly in toward the body of the bass as you pluck the string so that you're plucking both across and slightly downward.

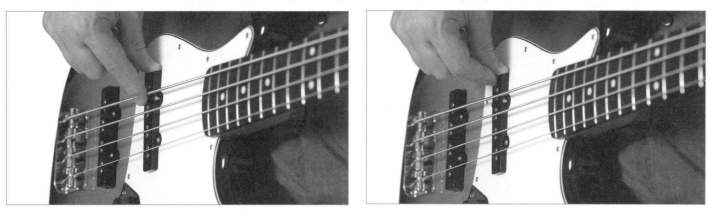

When plucking a string other than string 4, rest your thumb on string 4. Try plucking string 2 with your index finger. After plucking downward and through the string, let it come to rest against string 3.

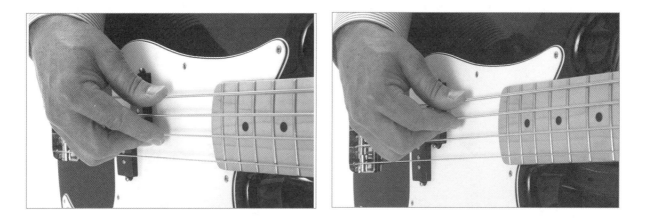

Playing with a Pick

Pick-playing is most common in rock styles. Picks come in all shapes, sizes, and thicknesses, so you'll probably want to go to a music store, buy one of several different kinds (it will only cost a few dollars), and try them out to see what you prefer. Hold the pick between your index finger and thumb. You don't need to strangle it, but make sure it doesn't come loose when you pick the string.

Most people pick from their wrist, though some people move their entire forearm. Try picking string 4 with a *downstroke*—that is, downward toward the floor. Don't use too much extraneous motion; the pick should either remain close to string 3 or come to rest against it.

Posture

If sitting, don't slouch and hunch over. Sit up straight and keep your shoulders and wrists relaxed. If standing, don't wear your bass around your knees! Keep the following tips in mind:

- When sitting, place and balance the bass on your right leg (unless you're a leftie).

- If you feel tension anywhere in your body, you most likely need to readjust. You should feel comfortable when playing.

- Tip the headstock slightly upward to make it easier for your fret hand to reach the notes.

- Don't lean the bass toward you to peek at the neck. Besides the fact that your bass will most likely have fret markers along the edge of the fretboard, you'll eventually want to be able to play without constantly looking at the notes.

Tuning

Tuning pegs are used to raise or lower the pitch of your bass strings. The image below illustrates which tuning pegs correspond to which strings.

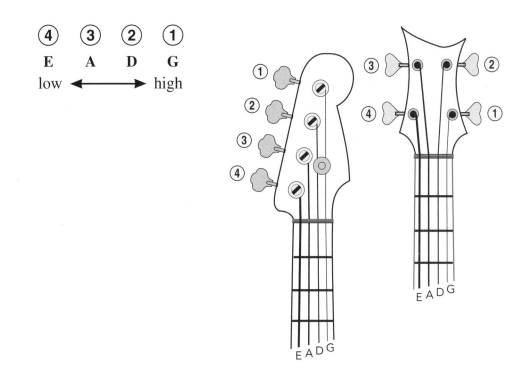

The process of raising or lowering the pitch of your bass guitar's strings is called *tuning*. When every string is adjusted properly, your bass is said to be "in tune."

🔊 Tuning pitches

For starters, match the open strings on your bass to the tuning pitches on the audio track. Of course, you won't always have access to a track of bass tuning pitches, so you'll need another way to tune your bass. Fortunately, there are several.

Electronic Tuner

One of the most common methods for tuning is using an electronic tuner. This is a device that can tell you whether your bass strings are sharp (too high) or flat (too low). They come in all shapes and sizes—and range in price from $5 to over $100—but they all do a pretty good job. If you can, try to purchase a *chromatic bass tuner*, as it will read any pitch—not just those of the open bass strings—and allow you to use it for various other instruments, should you need to do so. (Note that bass tuners are often combined with guitar tuners.)

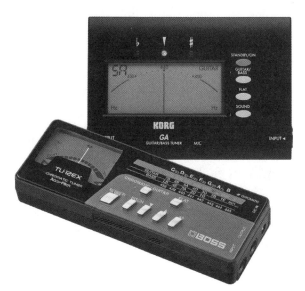

Piano or Keyboard

If you have access to a piano (that's in tune!) or a keyboard, you can also use them to tune your bass. See below for the notes on the keyboard that correspond with your bass's strings.

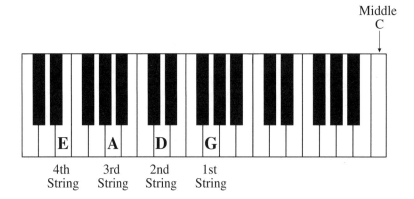

Relative Tuning

This involves tuning the instrument to itself, basically. It's an indispensable skill that you'll surely learn over time and is fabulous for developing your ear (i.e., improving your ability to hear and identify specific pitches). Here's how it works:

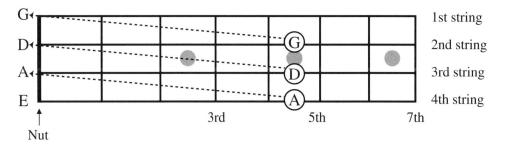

1. Tune string 4 to an E note by using a piano, pitch pipe, or any other available reference. If you have no available reference, estimate the pitch to the best of your ability.

2. Press string 4 down at the fifth fret and pluck the string. This is the note A. Tune the open third string to match this pitch.

3. Press string 3 down at the fifth fret and pluck the string. This is the note D. Tune the open second string to match this pitch.

4. Press string 2 down at the fifth fret and pluck the string. This is the note G. Tune the open first string to match this pitch.

Here are some important tuning tips, regardless of the method:

- Turn the pegs slowly at first, until you're comfortable with hearing the pitches change. You'll almost certainly need to pluck the string several times when tuning it at first.

- You'll hear a series of pulses, or waves, when matching a pitch. These are called *beats*. The closer the beats are together, the more out of tune the string is. As you get the string closer to matching the pitch, the beats will get farther apart. When they've disappeared altogether, the string is in tune.

- Always tune up to a pitch, rather than down to it. If you start tuning a string and discover that it's sharp (too high in pitch), begin by lowering it to where it's flat (too low), and then tune it back up to pitch. This will help the string stay in tune better in the long run.

10

Chapter 2
Explanation of the Notation Used in This Book

This book is designed to teach bass to those with no music-reading experience whatsoever. However, some form of notation is necessary in order to get across the concepts taught. Therefore, this book makes use of fretboard diagrams and a modified form of tablature, both of which are explained here.

Scale/Interval Diagrams

In Chapter 1, we briefly looked at the fretboard diagram; now let's take a closer look. These diagrams will be used to display scales, notes, intervals, and arpeggios (all of which will be discussed in subsequent chapters).

When we're dealing with open strings or notes within the first few frets, the nut will be included in the fretboard diagram. This diagram is telling you to play the note at the third fret of string 4:

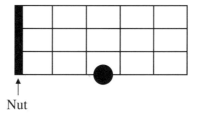

Open strings are indicated by a circle to the left of the nut. This diagram is telling you to play string 3 open (unfretted):

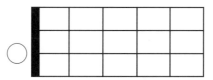

These diagrams are most often used to display a set of notes, such as an interval (two notes), a scale, or an arpeggio (which we'll cover later). In these instances, one note will usually be the *root*—the note from which the scale or arpeggio gets its name—and will be indicated by an open circle on the fretboard or, as an open string, a circle within a circle.

In the diagram below, the E notes (open fourth string and fret 2 of the second string) are the root notes. These two notes are the same, only the one on string 2 is one *octave* higher than the open fourth string.

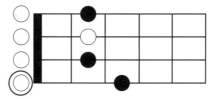

In this diagram, the G note at fret 3, string 4 is the root:

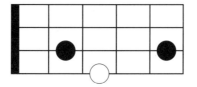

Eventually, we'll use diagrams that cover other areas of the neck, away from the nut. When that happens, a fret marker along the bottom will tell you where you are. In the following diagram, the fret marker tells us that the first fret of the diagram is fret 7. Therefore, the note at fret 8 of string 4 (which is the note C) is the root.

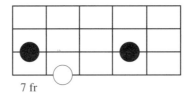

7 fr

You'll notice that your bass has fret inlays along the fretboard to help you keep track of where you are. Most often, these will appear at frets 3, 5, 7, 9, 12, 15, 17, and 19 (maybe more, depending on your bass). The marker at fret 12 is often different than the rest (a double dot, for instance), as the notes at that fret are exactly one octave higher than the open strings.

These fret markers normally appear along the upper edge of the fretboard, too, which helps make them visible even when you have your bass in playing position.

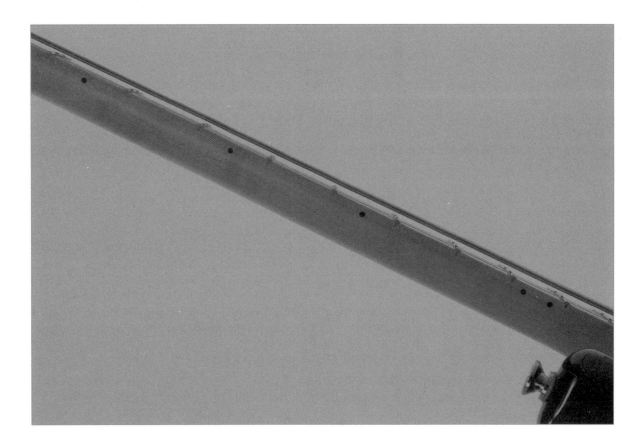

Tablature

Tablature, or "tab," is a notation system based on the physical properties of the instrument, as opposed to the musical pitches. The system has been around for almost a millennium, with its first documented use dating back to the 1300s. With regard to stringed instruments, such as the bass and guitar, tablature uses a set of horizontal lines to represent the strings. Bass tab has four horizontal lines—one for each string.

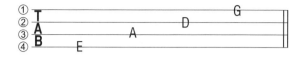

Open strings are indicated with a "0" written on the lines. This example tells you to play the open E string and then the open D string:

Other numbers indicate the exact fret location along the string. In this example, you'd play the third fret of string 4 and then the second fret of string 3:

Although it doesn't often happen on bass (as opposed to guitar, for example), if you see two (or more) numbers stacked vertically, you are to play them simultaneously. This example tells you to play the seventh fret of string 3 and the sixth fret of string 2 at the same time:

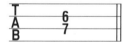

We normally play one note at a time on the bass; therefore, the tab will usually consist of a long string of individual numbers.

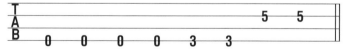

This is an easy system to read with regard to what notes to play and on what strings. The one detail it lacks is the *rhythm*. In other words, you can see what notes to play, but *when* do you play them? We have that covered, too. Read on!

Rhythm Notation

Rhythm makes up one half of standard notation. Whereas the pitches are represented vertically by notes on the staff, the rhythm is indicated by different noteheads and the stems attached to them. As mentioned, we're not going to use standard notation in this book; instead, we'll use tablature. But we're going to add to the tab by incorporating the rhythm element of standard notation. This notation is sometimes referred to as *rhythm tab* or *tab rhythm notation* and has become quite popular in the internet world of today.

Rhythm tab, just like standard notation, is read from left to right. The music is divided into *measures*, which are indicated by vertical lines, called *bar lines*, drawn through the staff.

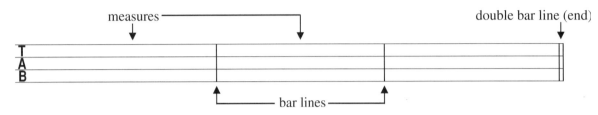

Just as with standard notation, each piece of music begins with a *time signature*, which appears right after the word "TAB" on the first staff of the example. A time signature consists of two stacked numbers. The top number tells you how many beats each measure contains, and the bottom number tells you what type of note is counted as one beat. The most common time signature is 4/4, which is also sometimes denoted by a "C," which stands for "common."

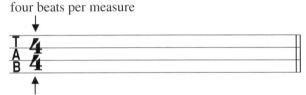

We use different noteheads and stems attached to the tab numbers to indicate different rhythms. The example below demonstrates different rhythmic values in a 4/4 time signature.

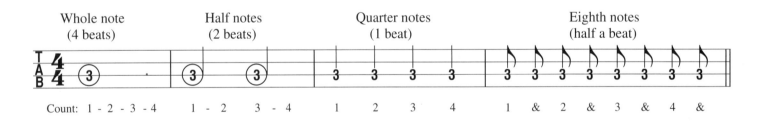

Notice that eighth notes look like quarter notes, but each one has a *flag* at the end of its stem. Normally, when several eighth notes appear in a row, the stems are connected with a *beam*. Also note in the following example that the direction of the stem depends on what string the note is on.

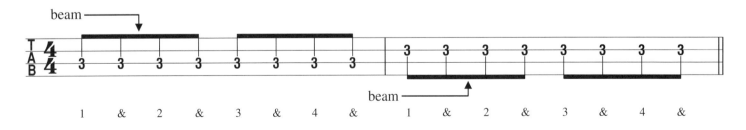

14

Of course, music does not only consist of notes; it also consists of silences—places where you don't play anything. This is called a *rest*, and we have different symbols for different rest rhythms, as well.

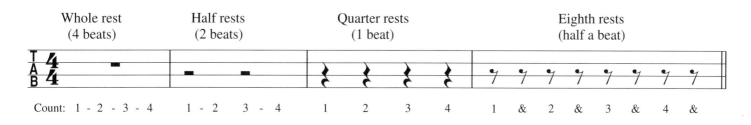

Unlike notes, though, there is only one kind of eighth rest. You normally won't see two or more eighth rests in a row; instead, you would use a larger-value rest.

So, instead of this: You'd see this:

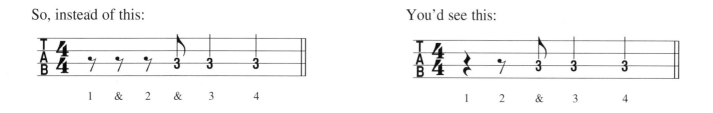

Check out the following examples to see some more rhythmic notation conventions. These aren't meant for you to play, obviously (although you will be able to by the time you finish this book!), but you'll absorb some basic concepts just by looking at them. You can try counting them, though!

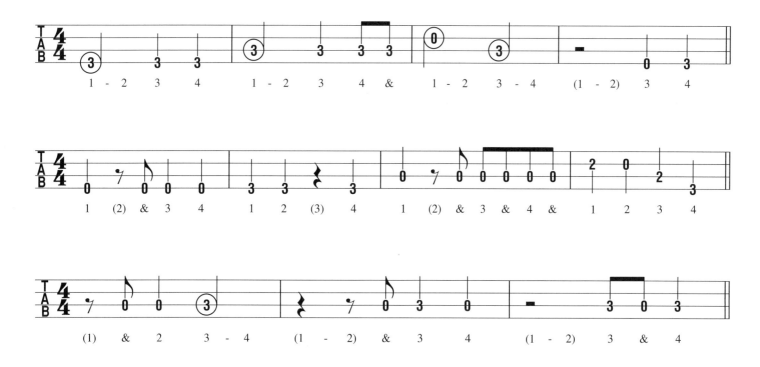

Chapter 3
Open-String Exercises

The purpose of this chapter is to develop the basic fingerstyle plucking technique in the right hand. We won't be using the left hand at all in this chapter, except for muting some strings at certain points to stop them from ringing out. It's very important to develop a good, solid plucking motion in the beginning of your studies, as this will allow you to progress more rapidly and with better tone.

Now let's try some open-string exercises, remembering the tips from Chapter 1:

- Keep your first knuckle (the one closest to the tip) straight as you pluck across and slightly downward, toward the body of the bass.

- Allow your plucking finger to come to rest against the next string when plucking strings 1, 2, or 3.

- Pluck with the pad of your finger—not the tip.

Example 1

Example 2

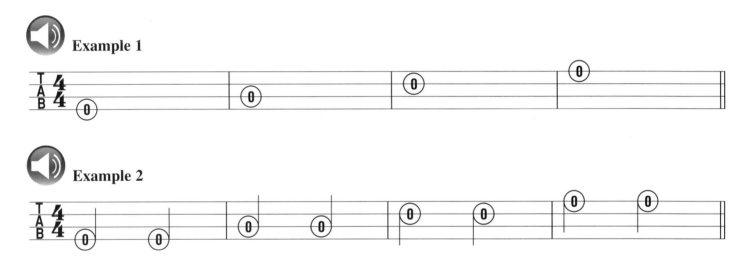

What's That Mess?

If you're wondering what that messy sound is when you move from the E string to the A string (and on up through the strings), then you're likely not doing one important thing: following through with your plucking finger and resting on the next string. When you pluck the E string and then move to the A string, the E string will keep ringing unless you stop it. This creates a low-frequency mess that doesn't sound very clean. By following through with your plucking finger and resting on the next string, not only does it keep your finger in close proximity to the strings for plucking the next note, but it also stops that string from ringing. So, if you pluck the E and A strings consecutively, your plucking finger should come to rest on the E string, thereby stopping it from ringing.

If you've been doing this already, congratulations on paying close attention and keep up the good work!

In this next example, we're going to encounter our first rests. This means that we'll need to stop the string from ringing before striking it again. We can do this one of two ways: with the plucking hand or with the fretting hand.

To stop the string with the plucking hand, simply replant the finger on the string—the same way you do when preparing to pluck the string the first time. So the order is:

1. Pluck the string.

2. Come to rest on the next string (if plucking strings 3, 2, or 1).

3. Replant the finger on the string when the rest occurs.

To use the fretting hand, simply lay your hand lightly across the strings—touching them without pushing them down to the fretboard.

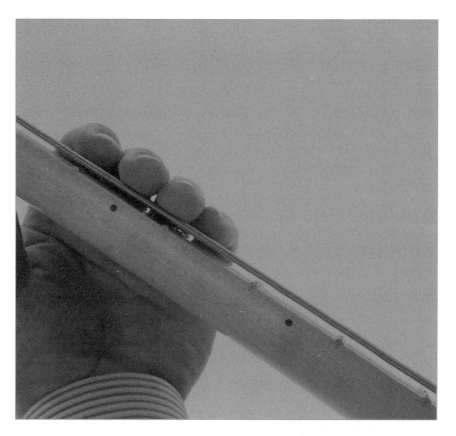

The safest bet is to use both methods (if possible), as this will ensure that the string will stop ringing cleanly.

Example 3

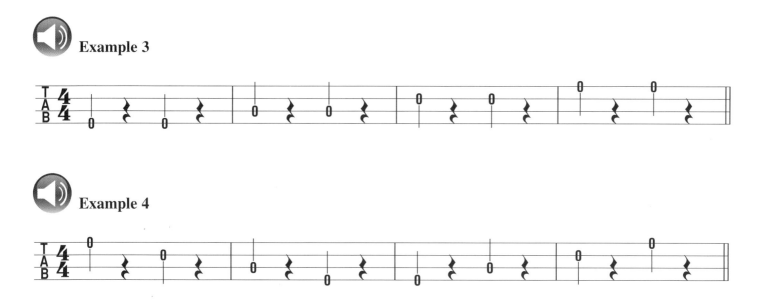

Example 4

OK, let's raise the bar just a little bit. We'll go back to sustained notes, but now we're going to skip strings when plucking. This means that, even though our plucking finger is coming to rest on the next string, it's not always going to stop the previous string from ringing—something else must be done. Let's take a look at the example.

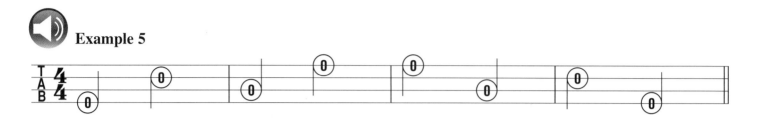

Example 5

Now let's examine this measure-by-measure to see what we need to do in order to keep the unwanted from ringing out.

> **Measure 1:** Right away, you have a problem: you pluck the E string and then pluck the D string. Your finger will come to rest on the A string after plucking the D string, but that won't stop the E string from ringing. If you were *really* paying attention at the beginning, you may have already been taking care of this problem. The solution? Plant your thumb on string 4. Whenever you pluck a string other than string 4, you should move your thumb off the pickup and instead plant it on string 4. This alone will take care of the ringing E string in measure 1.

> **Measure 2:** On beat 1, you need to stop the D string from ringing over. You'll need to do this with your fret hand. Lay your fingers lightly across the top two strings to stop the D string from ringing as you pluck the A string. However, after you pluck the A string, you pluck the G string and have to stop the A string from ringing out. The solution? Plant your thumb on the A string. This is the same move as in measure 1, only up one string. When you plant your thumb on the A string, it's a good idea to allow the nail front (the nail side) to touch the low E string, as well, since this will deaden it.

> **Measure 3:** After plucking the G string, you'll need to deaden it with the fret hand when you pluck the A string.

> **Measure 4:** When you pluck the D string, the follow-through will mute the A string. When you pluck the E string, you'll need to deaden the D string with your fret hand. This is just like the move in measure 3, only one string set lower.

Now go back and try the previous example again, making sure to follow these muting tips. You should end up with clean, distinct notes throughout the entire example.

Obviously, these aren't the most musically inspiring exercises, but mastering this chapter is imperative before moving ahead. Review it three, four, or five times if you have to, but make sure that you're able to play all the examples cleanly before moving ahead.

Chapter 4
Notes in Open Position

OK, now that you've got a handle on your right hand, it's time to start incorporating the left hand for more than just deadening strings. *Open position* refers to a location on the fretboard where your first finger is in line with the first fret. This is also sometimes called *first position*.

Now we're going to learn some notes that we can access while in open position.

String 4

As you know by now, the open fourth string is the note E. If we play fret 1 of string 4, we'll get an F note. Remember to press the string directly behind the fret—not on top of the fret and not too far back from the fret.

F Note on String 4

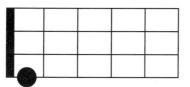

Let's try putting that note to use in a couple of examples. Remember what you learned in Chapter 3!

Example 6

Example 7

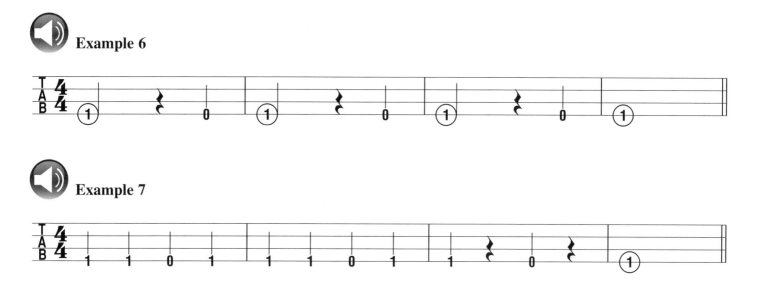

Don't "Fret" the Soreness

When you first start playing bass guitar, the finger tips of both hands are going to get sore. This is because they're being used in new and very specific ways and is perfectly normal. Eventually, you'll develop calluses on your finger tips and the soreness will go away. Depending on your practice routine, this could take weeks or months, but rest assured: the soreness won't last too long.

Now let's try another note. We'll play G with our fourth finger on fret 3 of string 4. You should also press down with your third finger (behind the fourth) whenever you can, just to add extra support. You can also play this note with your third finger if you'd like. If you do, go ahead and support it with your second finger. In fact, any time you play a note with a finger other than your first, it's a good idea to provide support with other fingers.

G Note on String 4

Example 8

Example 9

Faster, faster, faster!

It's a common misconception that playing slower notes is easier than playing faster notes. While it's true that more dexterity is required to move your fingers quickly and precisely, it's no easier to play slow notes *well* than it is to play fast notes. This means playing them right on the beat and not "rushing" ahead or "dragging" behind. To this end, a *metronome* is your best friend. This is a device that keeps perfect time for you at whatever tempo you select, whether slow or fast. Metronomes are relatively inexpensive and can even be downloaded for free as apps on your smartphone. Turn it on, set it to a slow tempo—say, 72 beats per minute—and try playing the examples in this book. It's guaranteed to help your "time" (your ability to play notes at the proper tempo without rushing or dragging).

In this next example, really concentrate on playing every note right on the beat and giving the rests their full duration.

Example 10

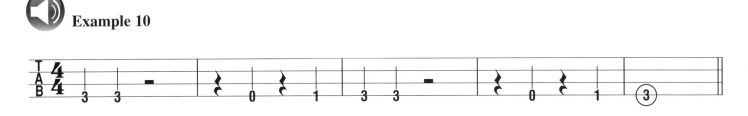

String 3

Let's move on to the A string now. Use your second finger to play fret 2 of string 3. This will produce the note B.

B Note on String 3

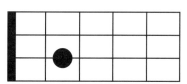

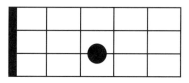 **Example 11**

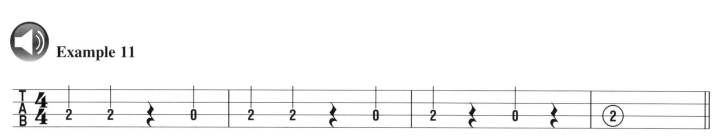

To play the C note on fret 3, use either your fourth finger (supported by the third) or your third finger.

C Note on String 3

> **Can You Spot the Dot?**
>
> When you see a *dot* next to a note, it increases the value of the note by one half. So, a *dotted* half note lasts for three beats, and a *dotted* quarter note lasts for one-and-a-half beats.
>
> $$\text{♩.} = \text{♩} + \text{♩}$$
>
> $$\text{♩.} = \text{♩} + \text{♪}$$

Don't rush!

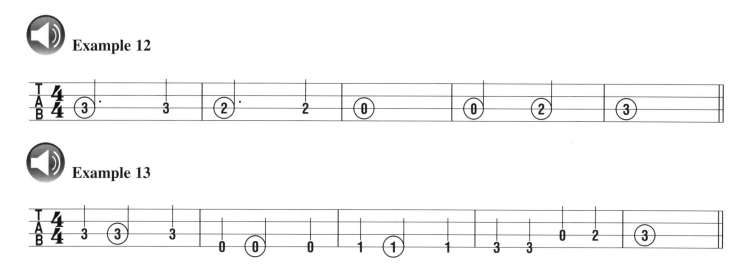 **Example 12**

Example 13

String 2

As you know, string 2 played open is a D note. Now try using your second finger on fret 2 to play an E note. This note is one octave higher than the open E (fourth) string.

E Note on String 2

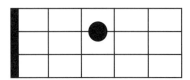

Now add the note F on fret 3 with either your third or fourth finger. This note is—you guessed it!—an octave higher than the F note on fret 1, string 4.

F Note on String 2

Pay attention to the rests here!

 **Example 14**

We're beginning to move from string to string a bit more quickly here. Make sure that you can perform this smoothly at a slower speed before playing it at tempo.

Example 15

This next song makes use of a 3/4 time signature. This means that there are three beats per measure, with the quarter note still getting the beat. To get a feel for this, listen to the audio track first and count along: "1–2–3, 1–2–3."

Example 16

String 1

The first string produces a G note when played open. To play an A note, use your second finger on fret 2. This is one octave above the open A (third) string.

A Note on String 1

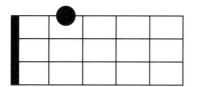

For the note B at fret 4, shift up the fretboard slightly and play it with your fourth finger. In fact, when playing the A note at fret 2 before or after this B note, you may want to just relocate to second position and use your first finger for the A note and your fourth (or third) finger for B.

B Note on String 1

The rhythm is a little tricky on this one, so listen first and count along!

Example 17

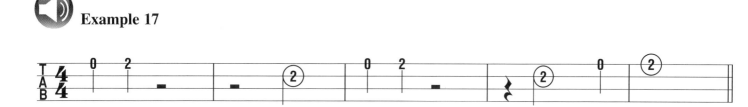

Be sure to cut off the notes for the rests in this one. There should be a full quarter note of silence in-between each note.

Example 18

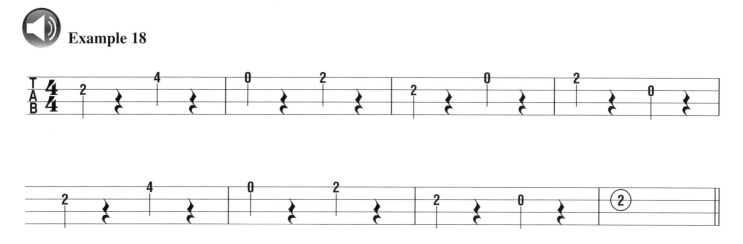

Song 1: Amazing Grace

Now let's put all that work to use with our first song: the gospel standard "Amazing Grace." This song is in 3/4 and uses mostly dotted half notes. Remember to plant your thumb on the E string when you pluck the open D string in measure 14, or else the E string will ring through, which won't sound good.

Note: The capital letters above the music are called *chord symbols*. We'll look at those in the next chapter.

What's Up with the Measure at the Beginning?

You'll notice that there's a measure at the beginning of the song with nothing but a quarter rest. This isn't an error; it's called a *pickup measure*, and it's there to account for the fact that this song doesn't begin on beat 1. If you sing this song, you'll notice that the word "amazing" begins before everything else. The "a-" is sung, and then everyone joins in on the "-mazing" part. So we say the "a" begins on beat 3 of the pickup measure, which is why there's a quarter rest there.

Note: The pickup measure is normally not included when counting measures; therefore, the first full measure is considered "measure 1."

Example 19
Amazing Grace

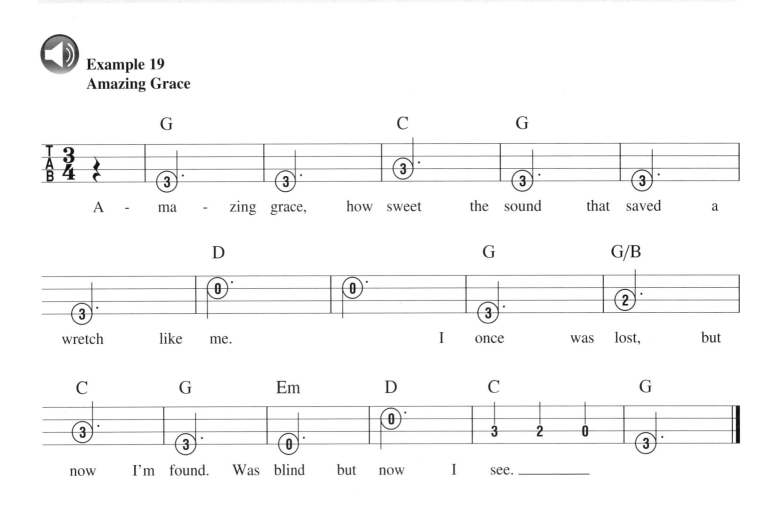

Song 2: Deep in the Heart of Texas

Now let's check out "Deep in the Heart of Texas." This song is in 4/4, and we're playing what's known as a *two-feel*. This means we play two notes every measure—typically, the root and 5th of the chord. We'll look at roots and 5ths a bit later in the book.

You have a few muting issues to deal with in this one—namely, the open D string. The first instance is in measure 4, where the open D is followed by the open A string. As you pluck the A string, you'll need to lay your left-hand fingers down on the D string to quiet it. When you play the G note at fret 3 of string 4 in measure 5, make sure that the underside of your fret-hand fingers is touching the A string so it will be muted, as well. The same can be said for the open D string in measure 7, where you play the G again.

In verse 2 ("The sage in bloom…"), notice that there are a few variations to keep it interesting. In measure 11, we go up to an E note on string 2 (the 3rd of C) instead of down to the 5th. In measure 15, there's a little walk-up on string 3 that connects the G to the C. This is a very common device.

Example 20
Deep in the Heart of Texas

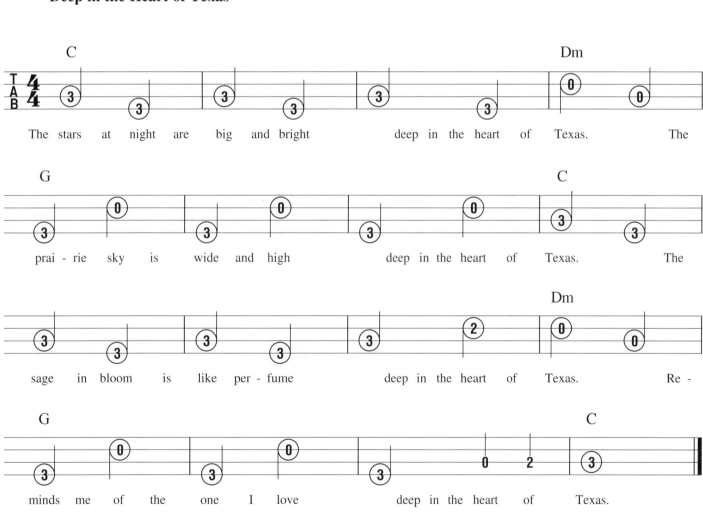

Song 3: E Minor Rock

Here's a rockin' tune in E minor that mixes in a fair share of rests. For each rest, remember to lay your left hand lightly on the strings to quiet them while your plucking hand prepares to pluck the next string.

> ### Major and Minor Keys
>
> Songs are said to be in a certain "key" because of the chords they use and which one feels resolved, or like "home." If a song is in a major key, the resolving chord—the one that feels like home—will be a major chord. Both "Amazing Grace" and "Deep in the Heart of Texas" are in a major key. This song, however, is in a minor key: E minor.
>
> Major songs tend to sound happy, bright, or uplifting, whereas minor songs sound dark or sad.

Example 21
E Minor Rock

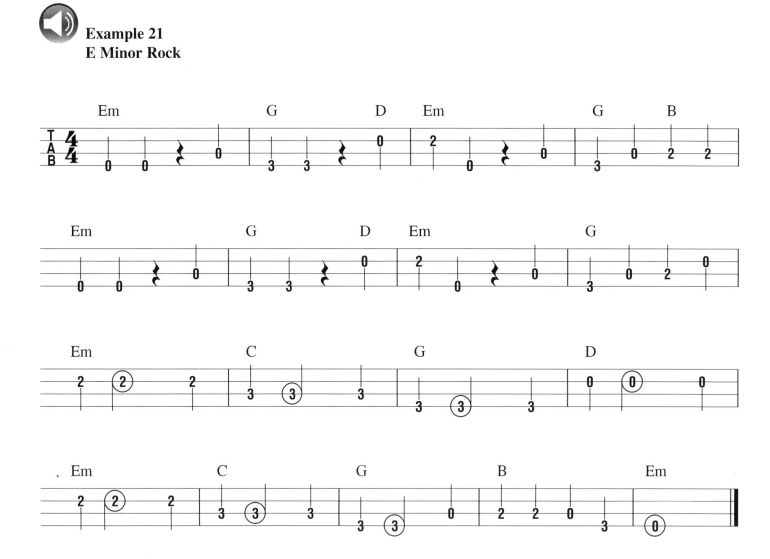

Chapter 5
Interpreting Chord Symbols and Musical Charts

Now let's give your fingers a bit of a break and exercise the ol' noggin a bit. As a bass player, we don't play chords very often—that's normally the job of the guitar player or keyboardist. However, it's very important that we know what chord symbols mean, because there will be times when you'll need to create a bass line on the spot with nothing more than a *chord chart*.

A chord chart—sometimes called a *lead sheet* or *fake sheet*—contains a melody, lyrics (if applicable), and chord symbols. In the professional arena, musicians are expected to be able to use a lead sheet to perform a song that they've never heard before (or at least don't know by heart). While this may sound daunting at first, once you have a few basic concepts under your belt, it's not nearly as bad as it sounds. As a bassist, the most important thing is the ability to understand chord symbols.

The simplest method for constructing bass lines is to just play the root of each chord in whichever rhythm seems to suit the song (listening to the kick drum can help out here!). As such, the bass lines in the two songs at the end of this chapter will solely consist of root notes. Other elements on a lead sheet include routing directions, repeat signs, and tempo markings. We'll look at each of these over the course of this chapter, but let's start with the all-important chord symbols.

Chord Symbol Nomenclature

If you see only a capital letter, then a major chord is implied. For example, if you see "C," then C major is implied; "D" means D major, etc. If you see a small "m" after the capital letter, such as "Cm," then a minor chord is implied. You may also see a minus sign ("C-") or perhaps "min" ("Cmin"). All of these symbols mean the same thing: minor. In the following example, we see chord symbols for C major, D minor, A minor, and F major. We also see repeat signs ‖———‖, which tell us to play through these four measures and then repeat them before moving on.

Note: Since they often contain a vocal melody or lead instrument melody, lead sheets often appear on treble clef. This isn't a problem, though, because we're usually only concerned with the chord symbols and the form of the song.

Sometimes you'll see *first and second endings*, as well. In the following example, you would do this:

1. Play to the repeat sign (through measure 4);
2. Go back to measure 1 and begin the repeat;
3. Play through measure 3, skip from the first ending (measure 4) to the second ending (measure 5), and then continue on.

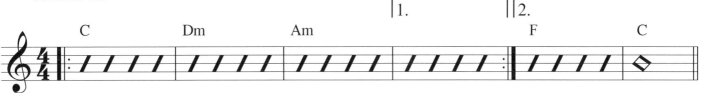

> **When Things Seem a Bit One-sided**
>
> Sometimes you'll come to an ending, or closing, repeat sign ‖ without having seen an opening one ‖. In this instance, you simply repeat from the very beginning of the song. It's for reasons such as this that it's always a good idea to quickly scan through a chart before trying to play it. This will allow you to catch these types of things and be prepared for them.

Chord Progressions

A *chord progression* is simply a series of chords strung together. The two examples on the previous page were chord progressions, as were the chords to the songs at the end of Chapter 4. There are certain chord progressions that are very popular and that are used all the time in pop, rock, blues, etc. One of the most popular is the I–IV–V progression. The Roman numerals here refer to chords built upon certain notes of a major scale. Let's look at this more closely.

Major Keys

As we briefly discussed on page 26, a song is either in a major key or a minor key. Major keys contain the same arrangement of chords, regardless of the tonic (the root note of the key). A major scale has seven different notes, and each one of those notes can have a chord built upon it. When using Roman numerals, we apply uppercase ones to major chords and lowercase ones to minor chords.

The arrangement of chords for any major key is as follows:

I   ii   iii   IV   V   vi   vii°

Note: The " ° " symbol after the vii chord stands for *diminished*, which is like a minor chord, but one note is different. You don't need to know much about the diminished chord right now, as major and minor chords are much more common.

The key of C, which contains no sharps or flats, is spelled: C–D–E–F–G–A–B. (C is the only major key with no sharps or flats; all other major keys require one or more sharps or flats.) Therefore, if we apply the above chord arrangement formula to this key, we'll get the following diatonic chords:

C   Dm   Em   F   G   Am   B°

I   ii   iii   IV   V   vi   vii°

Note: There are certainly times when you'll come across a chord other than these seven while in the key of C (B♭ would be a common one). These are referred to as *non-diatonic* chords, which is a can of worms too big to open in this book.

So, a I–IV–V progression in the key of C would contain C (I), F (IV), and G (V) chords. Make sense? Other common major-key progressions include the following:

I–V–vi–IV: (in C) C–G–Am–F

I–ii–iii–IV: (in C) C–Dm–Em–F

I–IV–I–IV: (in C) C–F–C–F

So what about other keys? Good question! Each major key has its own *key signature*—or collection of sharps or flats that it uses throughout the piece of music. The key signature for C major is blank, but every other major key will display one or more sharps or flats in the music. This is something that you'll eventually want to memorize, but for now, I'll just list them here for reference. Using this information, you'll be able to find the chords to any progression in any major key.

The 12 Major Scales

C Major: C–D–E–F–G–A–B	**F Major:** F–G–A–B♭–C–D–E
G Major: G–A–B–C–D–E–F♯	**B♭ Major:** B♭–C–D–E♭–F–G–A
D Major: D–E–F♯–G–A–B–C♯	**E♭ Major:** E♭–F–G–A♭–B♭–C–D
A Major: A–B–C♯–D–E–F♯–G♯	**A♭ Major:** A♭–B♭–C–D♭–E♭–F–G
E Major: E–F♯–G♯–A–B–C♯–D♯	**D♭ Major:** D♭–E♭–F–G♭–A♭–B♭–C
B Major: B–C♯–D♯–E–F♯–G♯–A♯	**G♭ Major:** G♭–A♭–B♭–C♭–D♭–E♭–F

Song 4: Chord Chart Rock in C

Here's a chart for a rock song in in the key of C major, along with a bass line that you might play if you were reading the chart. Notice that only the root note of each chord (the note from which the chord gets its name) is played. In addition to the repeat sign, we see another routing element: *D.S. al Coda* ("del segno al coda"). This is Italian and essentially means "from the sign to the Coda." When you reach this instruction, you go back to the "sign" (𝄋) and play until you see the "To Coda" instruction. At that point, you skip to the Coda section, which is indicated with the big crosshair symbol (⊕). This is simply a notational device that eliminates having to write out an entire section twice. Also notice the tempo indicator at the beginning of the song, which tells us that this song will move along at a moderate tempo. Sometimes you'll see a precise beats-per-minute (bpm) marking, such as ♩ = 120.

Example 22
Chord Chart Rock in C

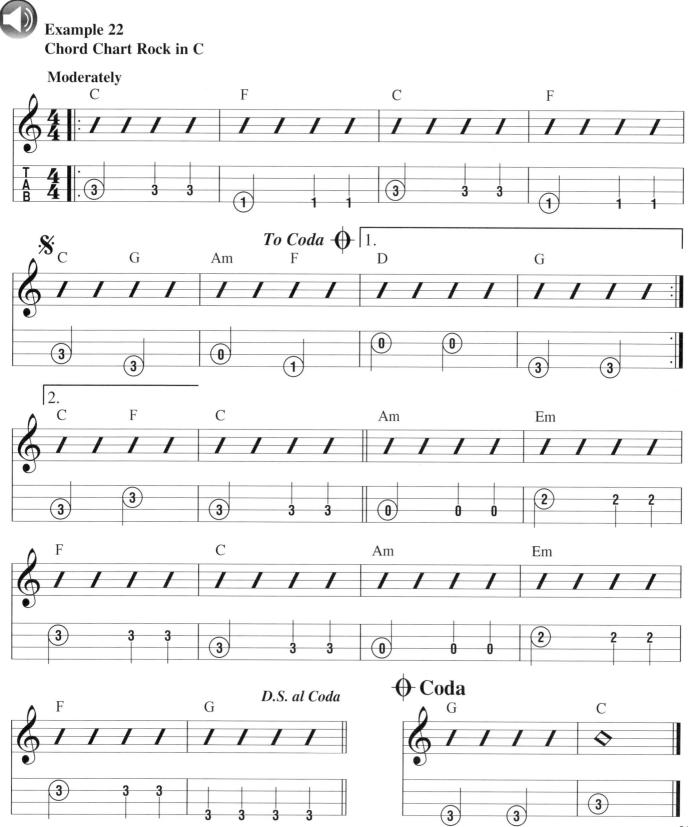

Song 5: Chord Chart Ballad in G

Here's a chart for a ballad in the key of G. You should be able to get through this one without many problems, but there's one new routing direction: D.C. al Coda ("da capo al coda"). This is Italian for "from the head to the coda." In this case, the "head" refers to the top—the beginning of the song. So, when you reach that instruction, go back to the beginning and play until you see "To Coda," at which point you jump to the Coda section.

Example 23
Chord Chart Ballad in G

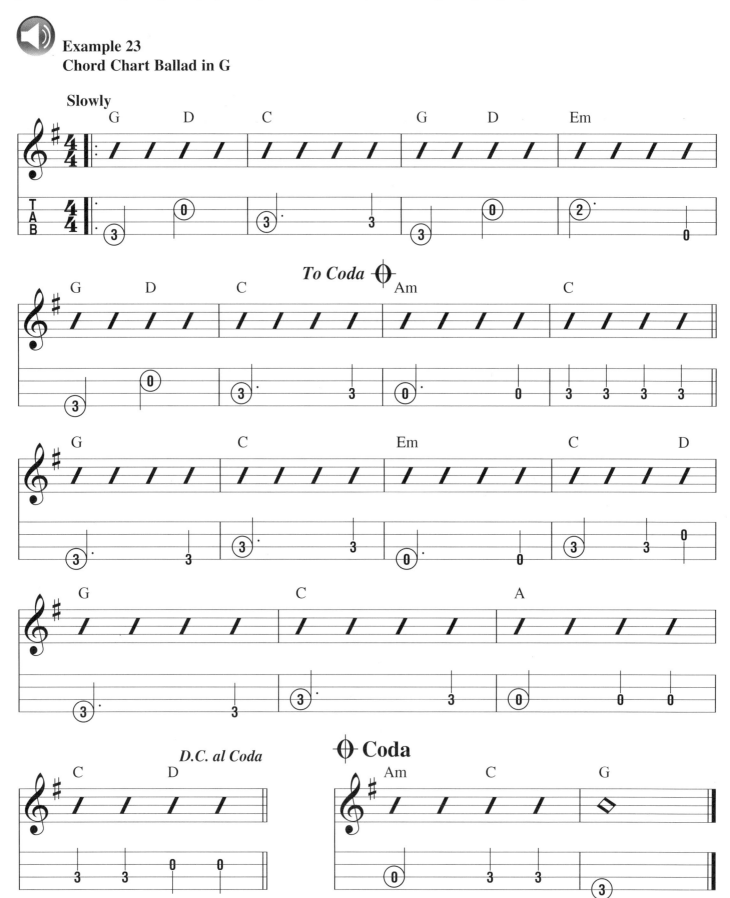

Chapter 6
Major Pentatonic Scales

All right, now let's get back to learning some more bass-specific things. In this chapter, we're going to learn one of the most useful scales in Western music: *major pentatonic*.

So, what is a scale, anyway? It's basically a collection of notes that we use to create melodies—and sometimes even chords. While most scales contain seven different notes, a pentatonic scale contains only five (hence the name: *penta* = five, *tonic* = tones). A major pentatonic scale is just like a major scale, except the fourth and seventh notes have been removed. By looking back at the table of major scales at the bottom of page 28, you should be able to figure out any of the 12 major pentatonic scales by simply deleting the fourth and seventh tones from each.

G Major Pentatonic Scale

Let's begin with the G major pentatonic scale, whose tonic (the note from which the scale gets its name, sometimes called the "root") is on fret 3 of string 4. This scale can be played in open position as follows (the extra A note on fret 2, string 1 is included because it's accessible within this scale form):

G Major Pentatonic Scale in Open Position

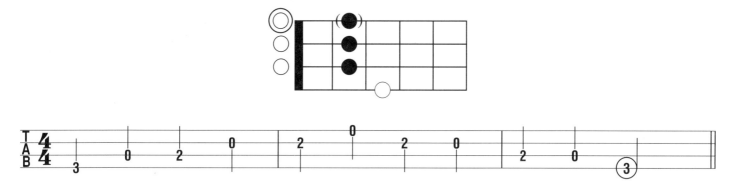

Play through the notes of this scale slowly at first, making sure that you're not allowing the open strings to ring out through subsequent notes. Once you have the fingering down, try these next examples:

Example 24

Example 25

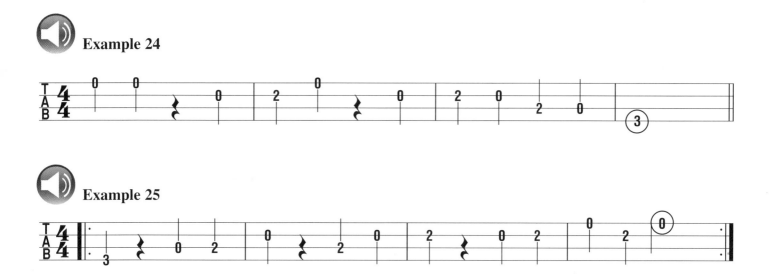

31

Alternating Fingers and the Rake Technique

Once we start playing eighth notes, you're most likely going to want to start alternating your first and second plucking fingers. When plucking, you should apply the same technique to your middle finger as you do to your index finger. The following example will help you get a feel for alternating your fingers in eighth notes. Try it with both of the suggested right-hand (R.H.) plucking fingerings (being able to lead with either finger when playing consecutive eighth notes is important). Start slowly at first and make sure that you're not rushing or dragging the beat.

 **Example 26**

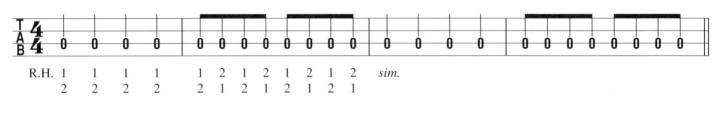

There's a technique that we use when descending from a higher-pitched string to a lower one—especially when playing eighth notes or really fast quarter notes—that makes it easier on your plucking hand and creates a smoother sound. It's called a *rake*, and here's how it works: whenever you pluck a note on one string and then immediately pluck a note on the lower adjacent string (the next thickest string—remember, we're talking about musical pitches, not physical geography), you use the same plucking finger to pluck both notes.

Let's look at a few examples to demonstrate this. First, we'll isolate the motion in repetition. Using the R.H. fingerings shown, play the following example slowly at first, gradually work it up to the speed on the audio track. The "rakes" are shown in the RH fingerings as horizontal connecting lines. Practice this example over and over until the rakes feel completely natural.

Example 27

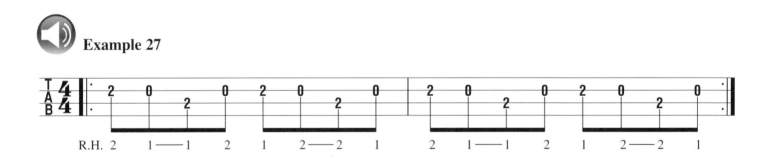

This next example is simply the G major pentatonic scale but, because we're playing in eighth notes, the rake technique is employed. Again, pay strict attention to and use both of the R.H. fingerings.

Example 28

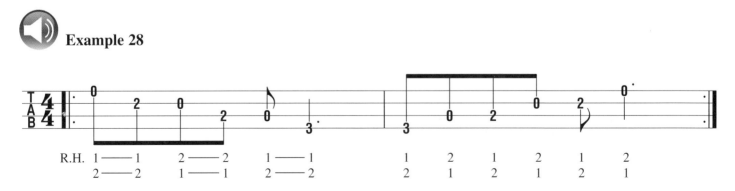

As you can no doubt see by now, descending requires much less energy in the plucking hand than ascending. This next example will really test you. Not only will you be making use of the rake technique, but you'll also be required to stop open strings from ringing with your fret hand.

- On beat 3 of measure 1, you'll need to stop the open G string.

- On beat 1 of measure 2, you'll need to stop the open D string.

- On beat 3 of measure 2, you'll need to stop the open A string.

Take this example very slow at first, making sure that you're getting it right in both hands before trying to speed it up to tempo. You need to be able to perform these maneuvers cleanly before progressing through the rest of the book.

Example 29

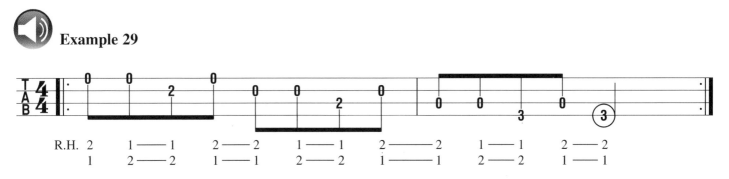

C Major Pentatonic Scale

Let's learn another major pentatonic scale before moving on. This one is in C. Since we're going to end up on fret 5 of string 1, it's best to just play this whole thing in second position. This means that you'll use your first finger for notes on fret 2, your second finger for notes on fret 3, and your fourth finger for notes on fret 5.

C Major Pentatonic Scale in Open/Second Position

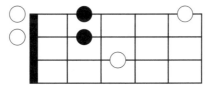

Let's put the scale to use in a riff.

Example 30

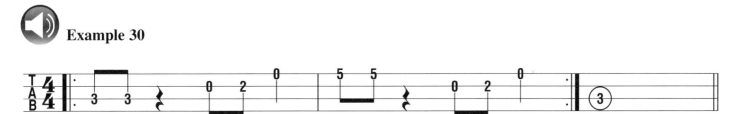

Song 6: G Blues Boogie

It's time to get down with a blues boogie. This song is based on the *12-bar blues* form, which is one of the most common (if not *the* most common) song forms in all of popular music. It's a 12-measure structure that makes use of the I, IV, and V chords of a key. We'll be using both the G major pentatonic and the C major pentatonic scales in this one, but, in measure 4, we sneak in an F note (fret 3, string 2) to make the G chord sound a bit bluesier.

There's also one new note in measure 11: E♭ (fret 1, string 2). Play this note with the first finger of your fretting hand.

E♭ Note on String 2

Be sure to stop the open D string from ringing on beat 3 of measure 9!

Example 31
G Blues Boogie

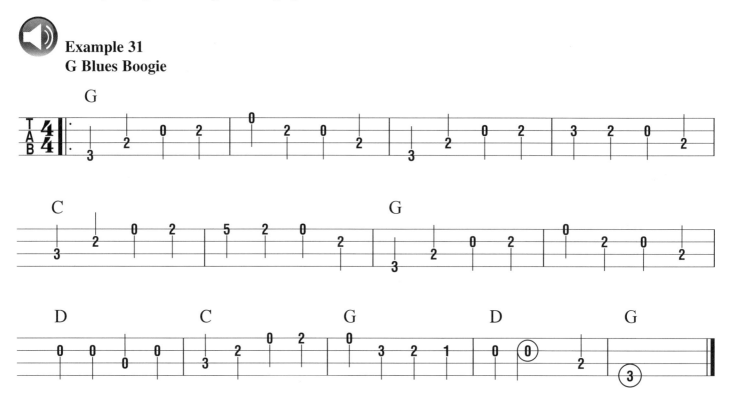

Song 7: C Major Pentatonic Motown

This is a Motown-style song that makes use of a repetitive C major pentatonic line. This is the fleetest-fingered example in the book so far, so take it slowly at first. It's much better to practice slowly and play it perfectly than to try to play it too fast and engrain bad habits in the process.

We have a new notational device in this song: the *staccato* marking. This is the dot that appears over the notes at the beginning of measures 5 and 6, and under the notes in measures 9 and 10. A staccato marking tells you to play that note in a short, clipped
manner. To make sure that you get a nice, clean staccato note, you should pluck the note and then immediately release fret-hand pressure while also planting your plucking finger on the string to deaden it. Try this out a few times before playing through the song.

Example 32
C Major Pentatonic Motown

Chapter 7
Minor Pentatonic Scales

The darker, more angst-ridden sibling of the major pentatonic scale is the *minor pentatonic scale*. It's a five-note scale, as well, but it's based on the minor scale, which we haven't looked at yet (we will in Chapter 9). However, that won't stop us, as we know what we need to know.

The minor pentatonic scale is created by omitting the second and sixth notes from the minor scale. It's often used in hard rock, blues, and funk styles, among others.

E Minor Pentatonic Scale

The E minor pentatonic scale can be easily handled in open position. Here's how it looks (the open G note and A note on string 1 are included because they're accessible within this scale form):

E Minor Pentatonic Scale in Open Position

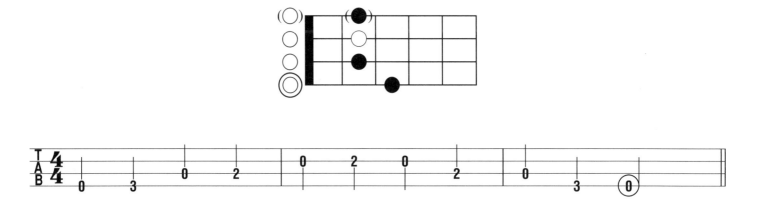

This scale should look familiar; it's an awful lot like the G major pentatonic scale, isn't it? There's good reason for that: E minor is the *relative minor* of G major. This means that the key of E minor shares the same key signature as G major: one sharp (F♯). Similarly, the G major scale (or G major pentatonic scale) shares the exact same notes as the E minor scale (or E minor pentatonic scale). The only difference is that, in E minor, the note E is treated as the tonic, whereas in G major, the note G is treated as the tonic.

Let's try it out in a few examples. Remember to make the rests distinct!

🔊 **Example 33**

🔊 **Example 34**

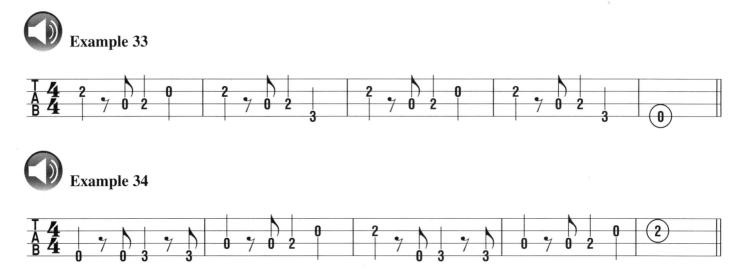

A Minor Pentatonic Scale

Now let's check out the A minor pentatonic scale, which looks just like E minor pentatonic, only up a string set (the open E note and G note on string 4 are included because they're accessible within this scale form).

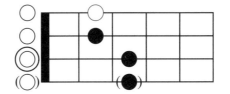

In case you were wondering: yes, this is the relative minor of C major. That's why it's so similar to the C major scale.

Here's how the A minor pentatonic scale sounds in some grooves. Be sure to use your fret hand to keep the open G string from ringing out in this first one.

Example 35

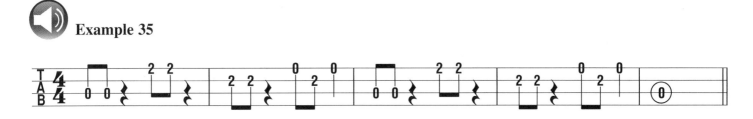

Here we have staccato notes again. Remember to plant your right-hand thumb on the A string to stop it from ringing when you pluck the high A on beat 2. Also remember to rake your plucking fingers on beats 3–4!

Example 36

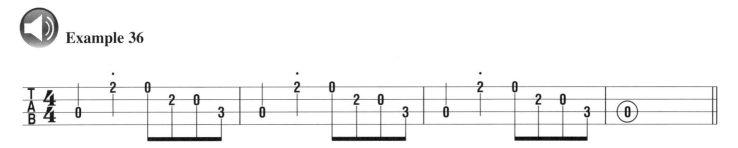

The notes below the tonic (open E and G notes on string 4) can sound really great when you include them.

Example 37

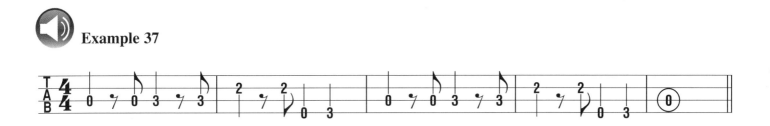

Song 8: E Minor Pentatonic Riff Rock

Here's a rocking tune in E minor that uses the E minor pentatonic scale exclusively. This one sounds best with a pick, so dig in! By the way: "N.C." (measure 9) stands for "no chord." There isn't an instrument playing a chord here—it's just a riff. The "G/B" symbol in measure 4 is a *slash chord*. This simply means that the bass is playing a note other than the root of the chord. In this case, the guitars are playing a G chord, but we're playing a B note. The B note is part of the G chord, however, which is why it doesn't sound terribly odd. We'll look more closely at that type of thing later in the book.

Example 38
E Minor Pentatonic Riff Rock

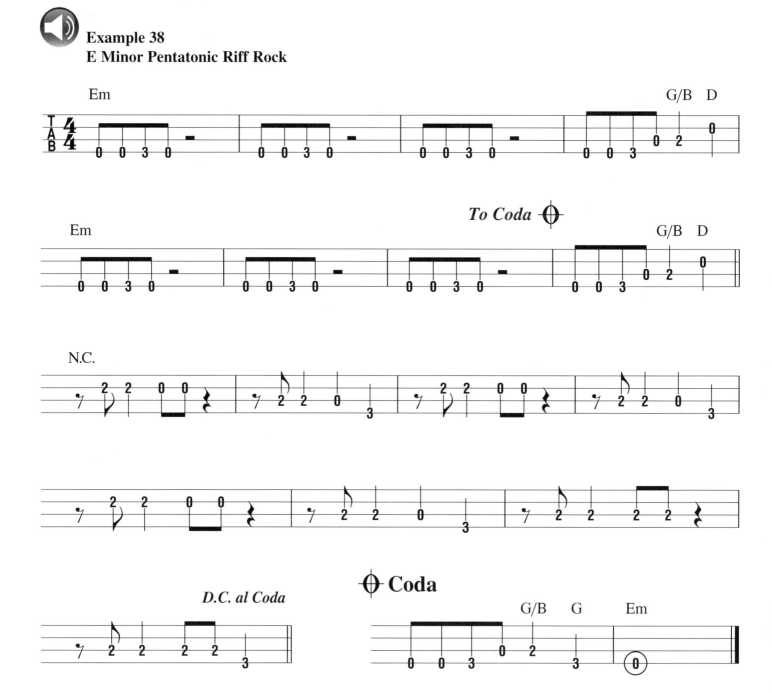

Song 9: A Minor Pentatonic R&B Groove

This song features a cool-sounding groove that uses our A minor pentatonic scale. Here are a few things to remember when working this one up:

- Use the rake technique when applicable. At the end of measure 2, you'll rake all the way from the G string to the A string with one smooth stroke!

- Note the staccato mark in measures 4 and 8 and the eight measures that follow.

- Tap your foot along while you play, as this will help to prevent you from rushing the beat.

- At the end of measures 1, 3, 5, and 7, you move from fret 2 of string 2 to fret 2 of string 1. When you do this, instead of refretting, simply "roll" your fret-hand finger from string 2 to string 1. You'll be playing string 1 with the pad of your finger instead of the tip. This technique will come in very handy as you move forward, so spend some time with it to make sure it feels natural. Consequently, if the order of the notes were reversed and you played string 1 before string 2, you'd need to plan ahead by fretting string 1 with the pad of your finger so you could then roll over to string 2 with the tip.

Example 39
A Minor Pentatonic R&B Groove

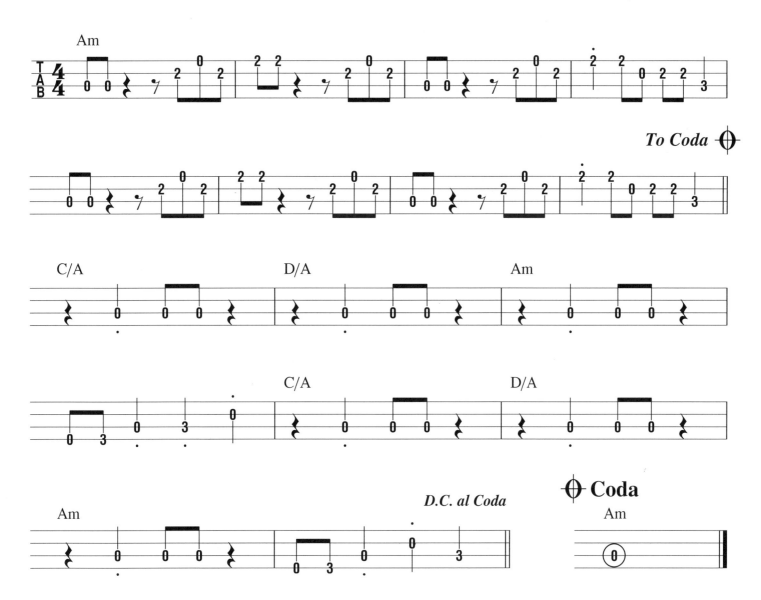

Chapter 8
Roots, 5ths, and Octaves

Take a few moments to pat yourself on the back at this point. You've come a long way, and you're starting to sound like a real bass player! If you haven't already done so, you should try to get together with some other musicians and jam a bit. Guitarist, drummer, keyboardist—just about anyone will do. It'll help you in more ways than you know, including pointing out the areas where you need the most work.

Technique Review

While we're on the subject of areas where you may need work, let's take a quick moment and review what we've covered thus far. Think of this as a "no technique left behind" checklist. Hopefully, you'll be able to check each one off and say, "Done! What's next?" If, however, you find that you're not doing one of these habitually, go back to the chapter where it's covered and review the material until it becomes engrained.

Left Hand (Fret Hand)

- Keep the thumb placed at (or near) the middle of the neck.

- Support the fretting fingers when possible.

- Keep open strings from ringing out (e.g., stop the open D string when you play the open A string).

- Roll your finger when moving to the same fret on an adjacent string.

Right Hand (Plucking Hand)

- Keep the first finger joint (closest to the tip) straight when plucking.

- Pluck across the string and slightly downward (into the body of the bass).

- When playing the low E string, plant the thumb on the pickup.

- When playing the A or D string, plant the thumb on the E string.

- When playing the G string, plant the thumb on the E or A string (to stop it from ringing out, if necessary).

- When moving from one string to an adjacent lower-pitched string, use the rake technique.

- Alternate the first and second plucking fingers when playing eighth notes.

OK, now that we've gotten that out of the way, and you've done your homework and are up to speed, we're ready to move ahead!

Interval Shapes

An *interval* is simply the musical distance between two notes (we've been playing all kinds of melodic intervals throughout the book). A *melodic interval* is one in which the notes are played in tandem (consecutively), whereas a *harmonic interval* is one in which the notes are played simultaneously. It's kind of like counting up the musical alphabet. For example, if we want to know the interval between the notes C and E, we simply count up from C:

C (1)–D (2)–E (3)

So, C to E is a 3rd because there are three note names involved. Now, there's a little more to it than that, and that's really only half the story, but we don't need to know everything just yet.

The intervals that we're interested in right now are 5ths and octaves, so let's talk about those.

The Root

As you recall, the note from which a chord gets its name is the *root*. (The note from which a scale gets its name is called the *tonic*, although it's sometimes called the root, as well.) Therefore, when we talk about intervals of chords, we're measuring them from the root. For example, if we have a C chord, then C is the root.

The 5th

When we talk about the 5th of a chord, we're simply talking about the note that is five note names above the root. We learned earlier that from C to E is a 3rd because there were three note names involved: C, D, and E. Another way to say this is that E is the 3rd of a C chord. So, can you guess what the 5th of a C chord would be? If you said "G," you're absolutely correct.

C (1)–D (2)–E (3)–F (4)–G (5)

So why are we talking about this? Well, it just so happens that the 5th of a chord is a very strong note, one that we can use when creating our bass lines. On the bass fretboard, a 5th looks like this on adjacent strings (R = root, 5 = 5th):

Interval of a 5th—Adjacent Strings

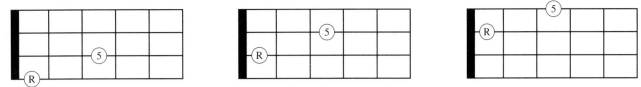

And on non-adjacent strings, it looks like this:

Interval of a 5th—Non-Adjacent Strings

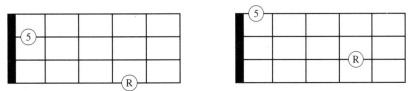

These are moveable shapes, meaning they can be slid anywhere up or down the neck. Of course, these can be played in open position, as well. A 5th based off the E string would look like this:

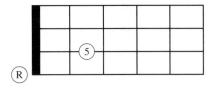

The Octave

An *octave* is simply two notes of the same name, with one note either higher or lower in pitch. It's easiest to see on a piano keyboard because the same order of keys repeats over and over throughout the range of the instrument. If you play middle C and then play the C to the left of that, you're playing one octave lower. Here's what a moveable shape of an octave looks like on the bass (R = root, O = octave):

Interval of an Octave—Spanning Three Strings

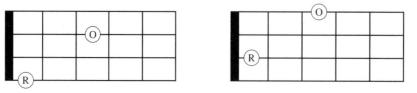

And another possibility, though less common, spans all four strings.

Interval of an Octave—Spanning Four Strings

And an octave shape based off the open A string would look like this:

We often make use of these shapes (5ths and octaves) when creating bass lines. In fact, many of the bass lines thus far in the book have done this.

Fretboard Note Chart

Speaking of creating bass lines, let's take a look back at the idea of creating a bass line from a chart. Armed with your new knowledge of roots, 5ths, and octaves, you're on your way to improvising usable bass lines. Before we can make use of these moveable interval shapes, however, we need to learn the names of the notes further up the neck.

I don't expect you to learn all of these right away; they're presented here as a reference that you can use when you see a chord symbol. It's best to start with just the E string and A string. After that, you can use the octave shape (two strings over and two frets up) to learn the D and G strings.

Notes on the Fretboard—E and A Strings

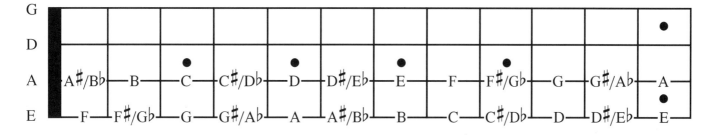

Realize that many of these notes can be played in several places. For example, the C note at fret 8 of string 4 is the same note as the one you already learned at fret 3, string 3. And the D note at fret 5, string 3 is the same note as the open D string, etc.

Two Names for One Note?

You no doubt noticed in the diagram above that some frets had two note names assigned to them. These sharp/flat notes are equivalent to the black keys on the piano. The white keys on the piano spell a C major scale, which, if you remember, contains no sharps or flats. The black key notes in-between can be viewed in one of two ways: as higher than a white key (sharp) or lower than a white key (flat).

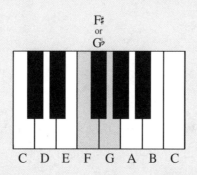

Whether a note is called a "sharp" or a "flat" depends on a few things, the most prevalent being what key you're in. If you're playing in the key of D major, which is a sharp key, then the note between F and G would be called F♯; if you're playing in the key of D♭, which is a flat key, then that same note would be called G♭. By the way, the word for one note having two names is *enharmonic*. In other words, F♯ and G♭ are said to be "enharmonic."

Don't worry too much about these sharp and flat notes at this point—we won't make much use of them. But it's good to be exposed to this concept, as you'll no doubt encounter it in your studies before too long.

Common Rhythmic Patterns

Now that you know the names of the notes on the low strings (or at least can reference them), we can begin to use our roots, 5ths, and octaves to create simple bass lines from chord charts. Let's take this basic root–5th–octave shape and use it to generate some bass lines that employ common rhythmic patterns:

Root–5th–Octave Shape

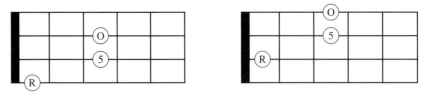

Pattern 1

Let's start with a simple pattern that uses quarter notes and half notes. We'll make use of only root notes here, simply moving them along the E and A strings to match the root of each chord. Regarding the fret hand, you can use whichever fingering feels best for now. Notice the staccato marks on beat 1!

Example 40

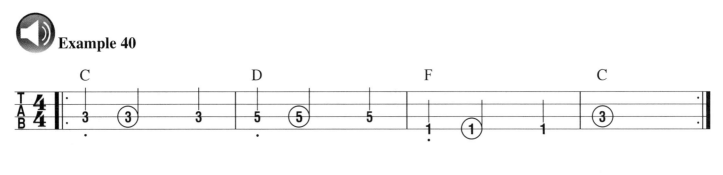

Pattern 2

This is a nice pattern with a nice bounce. We'll use the root and 5th for this one, with all the roots located on the fourth or third strings.

Example 41

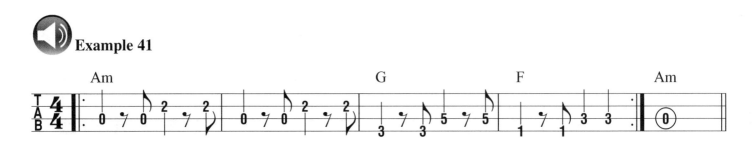

Pattern 3

$|\frac{4}{4}$ ♫ ♪ ♫ ♪ $\|$

This is a powerful rhythm that uses short bursts of eighth notes. Remember to alternate your plucking fingers. We'll be using the root/octave approach here, including both the 4/2 string shape and the 3/1 shape.

Example 42

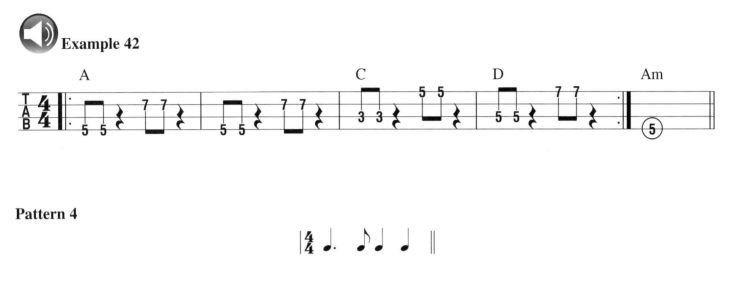

Pattern 4

$|\frac{4}{4}$ ♩. ♪ ♩ ♩ $\|$

This pattern combines dotted quarter notes, eighth notes, and regular quarter notes. We'll be using the same root–5th–octave pattern for each chord and simply moving it down the neck.

Example 43

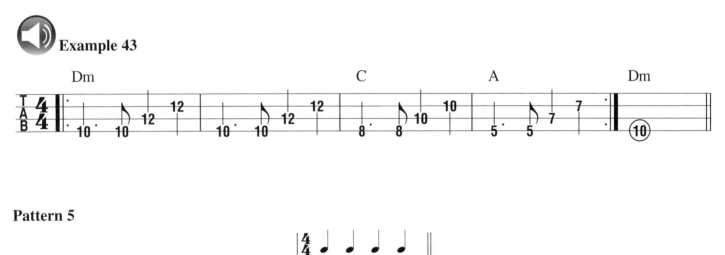

Pattern 5

$|\frac{4}{4}$ ♩ ♩ ♩ ♩ $\|$

This pattern consists of nothing but quarter notes and is great for a "walking" bass style. We'll use a root–octave–5th–root pattern here. Remember to rake the strings!

Example 44

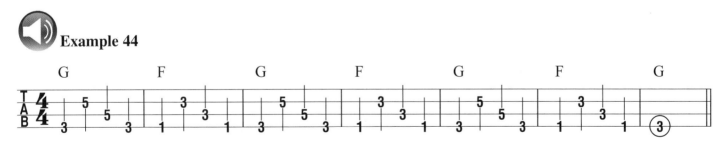

Chapter 9
Major and Minor Scales

Now let's flesh out our five-note pentatonic scales and learn the full, seven-note major and minor scales. We briefly looked at the majors on paper (page 28), but now we'll learn how to play a few of them. Major and minor scales are by far the two most common in all of Western music.

G Major Scale

We'll play the G major scale in open position, but we'll have to learn one new note, F♯. Remember from page 28 that the key signature for G major is one sharp: F♯. (The extra notes below the root, open E and F♯, and above the octave, A and B, are included because they're accessible in this form.)

G Major Scale in Open Position

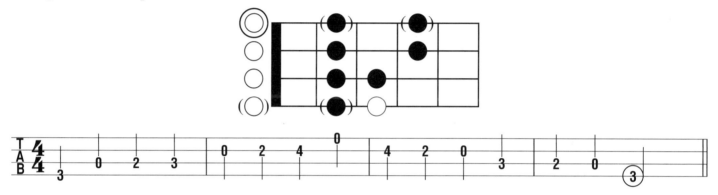

Those half steps (the distance of one fret) can be used to great effect as lower-neighbor tones in grooves like this:

 **Example 45**

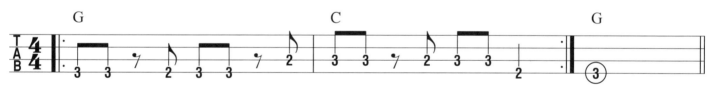

C Major Scale

As with the C major pentatonic scale, we'll play this one in second position (first finger on second fret). Even though it uses some open strings, the scale ends up at fret 5 and we don't need to play fret 1. (The notes below the root are included because they're accessible in this form; you will have to shift down a fret for the F note on fret 1, string 4.)

C Major Scale in Open/Second Position

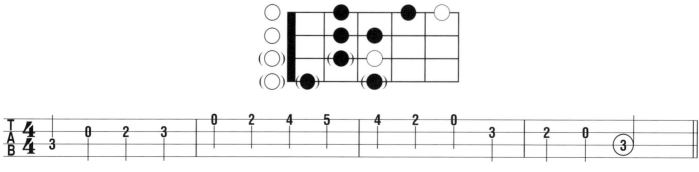

Let's check out the C major scale in use. Note that this one's in 3/4 time. The little scale runs in measures 4 and 10 are extremely common.

Example 46

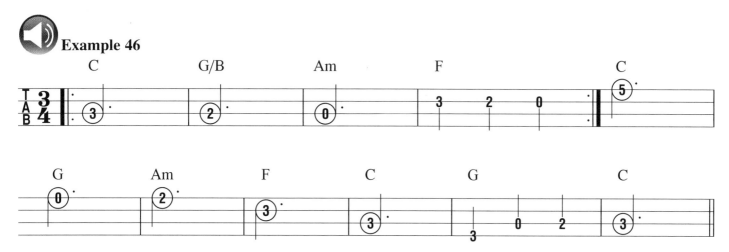

E Minor Scale

Now let's turn to the dark side with the E minor scale in open position. Again, as with the pentatonic version, this will bear great resemblance to the G major scale—the only difference being which note we treat as the tonic. (The notes above the octave are included because they're accessible within this form.)

E Minor Scale in Open Position

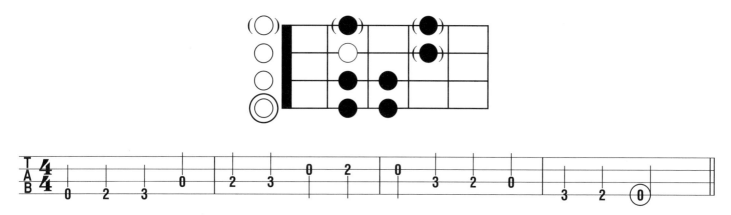

Now let's check out the E minor scale in action. We're using some *passing tones* here—notes that we pass through on the way to another destination note.

Example 47

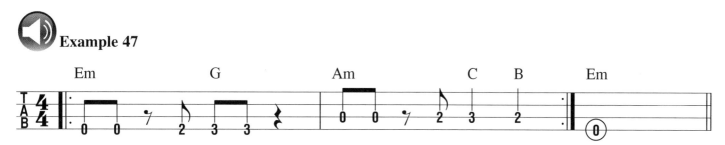

A Minor Scale

Here's the A minor scale in open position, which looks just like the E minor scale, only one string over. The notes below the root are included because they're accessible within this form.

A Minor Scale in Open Position

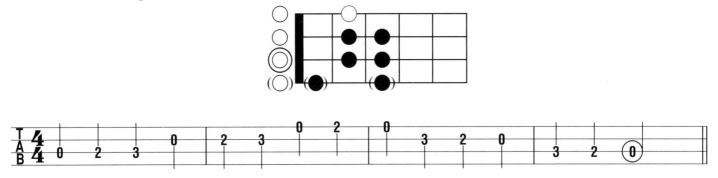

Here's the A minor scale in a groove. Note that this is essentially just a descending minor scale, but we're phrasing it in such a way that it creates a nice bass line. Remember to observe the rests!

Example 48

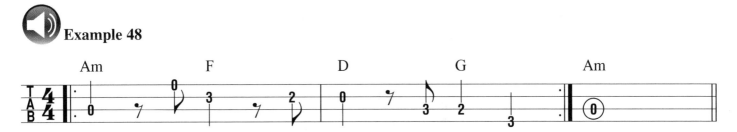

Just as we did with the major scales on page 28, all 12 minor scales are listed here for reference:

The 12 Minor Scales

A Minor: A–B–C–D–E–F–G	**D Minor:** D–E–F–G–A–B♭–C
E Minor: E–F♯–G–A–B–C–D	**G Minor:** G–A–B♭–C–D–E♭–F
B Minor: B–C♯–D–E–F♯–G–A	**C Minor:** C–D–E♭–F–G–A♭–B♭
F♯ Minor: F♯–G♯–A–B–C♯–D–E	**F Minor:** F–G–A♭–B♭–C–D♭–E♭
C♯ Minor: C♯–D♯–E–F♯–G♯–A–B	**B♭ Minor:** B♭–C–D♭–E♭–F–G♭–A♭
G♯ Minor: G♯–A♯–B–C♯–D♯–E–F♯	**E♭ Minor:** E♭–F–G♭–A♭–B♭–C♭–D♭

Song 10: The Star Spangled Banner (Bass Line in G)

Are you ready to do your country proud? Here, we'll tackle a bass line to the "Star Spangled Banner" in the key of G. Every note here comes from the G major scale, with the exception of two: D♯/E♭ on fret 1, string 2 and C♯ on fret 4, string 3. So be on the lookout for those notes, and be sure to stop any open strings (namely, the D string) from ringing out longer than it's supposed to.

Example 49
The Star Spangled Banner (Bass Line in G)

Song 11: The Star Spangled Banner (Melody in C)

Now we'll play the melody to the "Star Spangled Banner" on the bass. We'll transpose it to the key of C to better fit the range of our bass, and we'll have to transpose a few phrases to a different octave (the song has quite a range!), as well, but the essence will remain. The only note here that's not in the C major scale is the F# on fret 2, string 4, which appears in measures 3, 11, and 23. You can play this entire song comfortably in second position.

Example 50
The Star Spangled Banner (Melody in C)

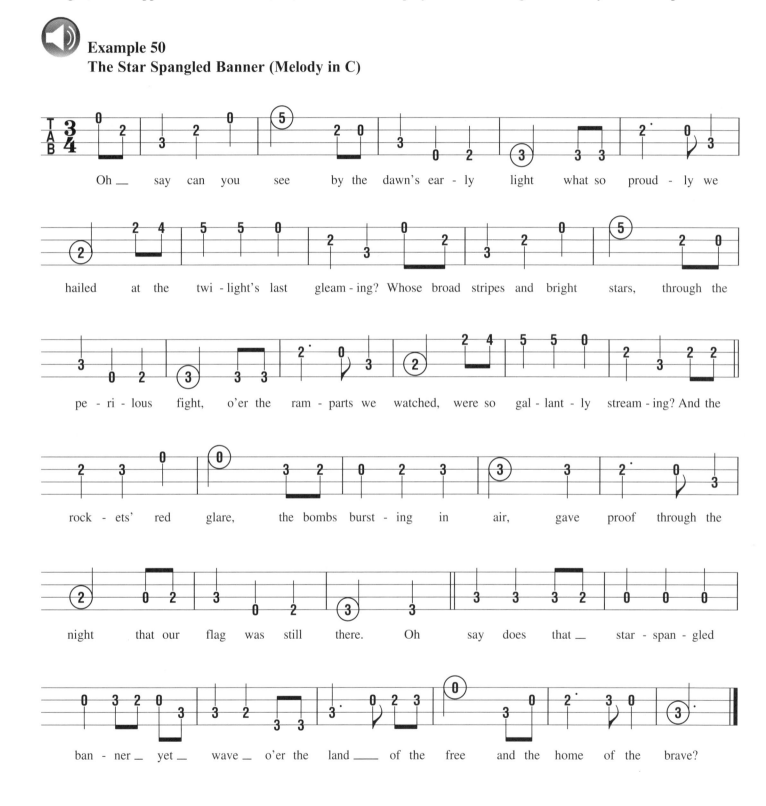

Chapter 10
Moveable Arpeggio Shapes

We're going to close things out with a look at some more incredibly useful moveable shapes: arpeggios. What's an arpeggio? Glad you asked (it means you're paying attention)! An *arpeggio* is simply the notes of a chord played separately, or one after the other. A *triad*, for example, is a chord containing three different notes. A C major triad contains the notes C, E, and G (the root, 3rd, and 5th). If we played those notes one after the other, we'd be playing a C major arpeggio. It turns out that these notes—the root, 3rd, and 5th—are great for building bass lines, and that's our aim here. Just as we used the root/5th/octave shape to create bass lines in Chapter 8, in this chapter, we'll be doing the same with moveable arpeggio shapes. Reference the fretboard chart on page 43 when you need to.

Major Triad Shape

As we said earlier, a major triad contains a root, a 3rd, and a 5th. (Technically, the 3rd is a *major 3rd* because it's derived from the major scale, and the 5th is a *perfect 5th*, but that's not terribly important right now.) By far the most common major triad arpeggio shape on the bass involves two strings and looks like this:

Two-String Major Triad Shape

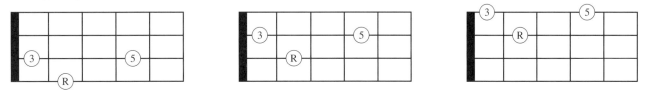

Let's check out what this shape can do when applied to some of the common rhythmic patterns from Chapter 8. This example uses rhythm pattern 4 and transposes the line from the G chord to the C chord:

Example 51

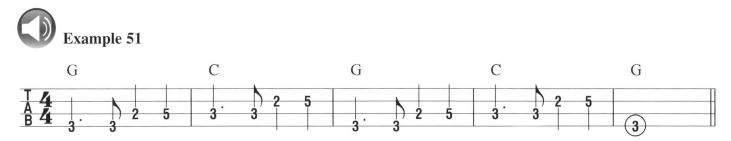

And here's a walking-style line in C that uses rhythm pattern 5 for F, C, and G chords. Notice that we break away from the arpeggio in measure 4 and walk back up to F to keep things from getting too predictable.

Example 52

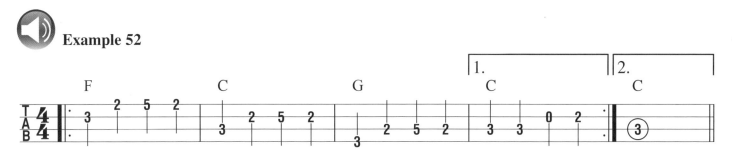

Minor Triad Shape

A minor triad contains a root, a ♭3rd, and a 5th. So, in order to make a major triad a minor one, we need to lower the 3rd by a half step (to a *minor* 3rd). At the top of the next page is a common shape involving two adjacent strings:

Two-String Minor Triad Shape

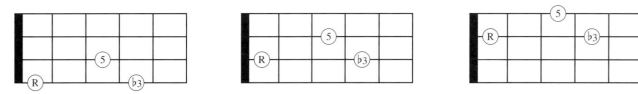

Here's an E minor line that uses this shape for Em and Am chords and incorporates rhythm pattern 3, as well. Note that, although we're using the open strings here, it's still the moveable shape; it's just that the open string (the nut) is acting as the low root.

Example 53

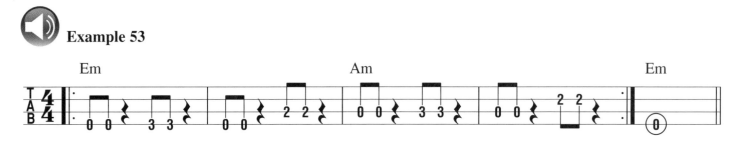

This example uses rhythm pattern 1 to create a bass line with the B minor triad shape and the A major triad shape. Notice that you can jumble up the notes a bit and still convey the tonality; you don't have to play straight up or down through the shape.

Example 54

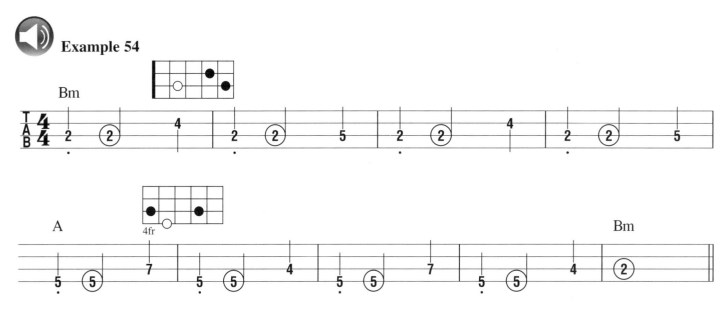

In addition to triads, another common chord type is the *seventh chord*. This is a four-note chord that not only contains the root, 3rd, and 5th, but also—you guessed it!—the 7th. There are many different kinds of seventh chords, but we'll focus on the two most common here: dominant seventh and minor seventh.

Dominant Seventh Shape

A dominant seventh chord is like a major triad but with a minor 7th interval on top. In other words, you use the 3rd from a major scale but include the 7th from a minor scale (the 5th is the same in both). (Refer to the charts on pages 28 and 48.) So, a C7 chord contains the notes C, E, G, and B♭. E is the 3rd of the C major scale, and B♭ is the 7th of the C minor scale.

Since we're going all the way up to the ♭7th anyway, we'll extend these shapes up to the octave root. Here's the most common shape, which spans three strings:

Three-String Dominant Seventh Shape

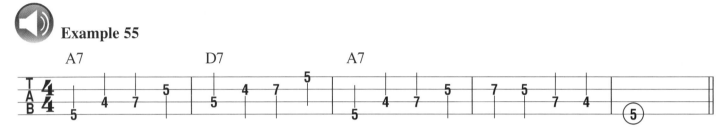

With four notes and four beats in a measure, this shape is tailor-made for a quarter-note walking line (rhythm pattern 5). Here's an example that uses A7 and D7 shapes in fourth position:

Example 55

And here's one in C that uses rhythm pattern 4. We're in second position here.

Example 56

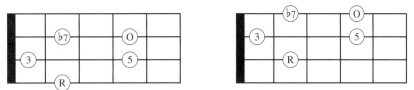

Minor Seventh Shape

A minor seventh chord is like a dominant seventh chord but with a minor 3rd instead of a major 3rd. So, a Cm7 chord contains the notes C, E♭, G, and B♭. Here's a common three-string shape:

Three-String Minor Seventh Shape

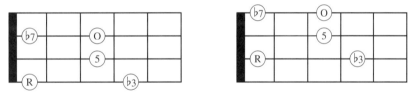

Here's an example that uses the open-position E minor version of this shape (the nut acts as the low root and ♭7th) and rhythm pattern 5. This is another example of jumbling up the notes a bit.

Example 57

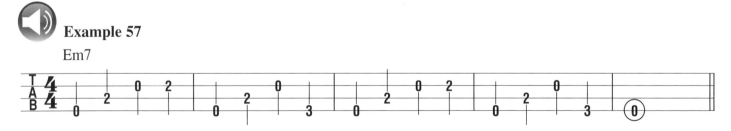

We'll finish up with one in C minor that uses rhythm pattern 2, again jumbling up the notes a bit.

Example 58

Song 12: Bluesy Shuffle in A

This song features a *shuffle beat*. This means that the eighth notes aren't played evenly; the first one in each beat is longer than the second. You've heard this in countless songs, and after listening to the audio track once, it will immediately become familiar to you. You only play a few eighth notes (for the A7 chords) in this whole song, so it won't even matter most of the time (quarter notes sound the same in a shuffle as they do in a "straight eighths" song).

We're mixing a few different arpeggio shapes here: A7 for the A7 and most of the D7 for the D7 chords (though a different pattern), and an E triad for the E7 chord. We also follow the E major triad with a D major triad. Note that, even though we're playing E major and D major triad shapes in measures 9 and 10, the chords played by the guitar are still E7 and D7, respectively, hence the chord symbols. Once you get the basic quarter-note routine down, then you can start to add in the eighth-note variation on the A7 chord in the second half of the tune, which just helps it "swing" a bit more. Remember to use the rake!

Example 59
Bluesy Shuffle in A

54

Song 13: Final Exam Rock in E Minor

This is called "Final Exam Rock" because it brings together many concepts that we've studied throughout the book. Let's break it down by measure:

- **Measures 1–4:** This section is based on an Em7 arpeggio form. Remember to rake from string 3 to string 4 at the end of each two-measure phrase.

- **Measures 5–6:** We're using the root/5th approach here for the C and B chords. The open A string is used at the end of measure 5 as an approach tone to B. Again, be sure to rake from the 5ths (on string 2) to the roots (on string 3).

- **Measures 9–10:** This line is built from notes of the E minor scale. The only note not included in the ascent is C. At the end of measure 10, we have a three-string rake (!): the open D string, the note B (fret 2, string 3), and the open E string. All three of these notes should be plucked by the same finger in one continuous motion.

- **Measure 14:** Here, we continue scaling up the higher register of the E minor scale.

- **Measures 15–17:** Here, we have a repetitive four-note motif. Once again, the important thing is to rake. Pluck the first two notes (beat 1) with one finger and the next two notes (beat 2) with the other finger.

Example 60
Final Exam Rock in E Minor

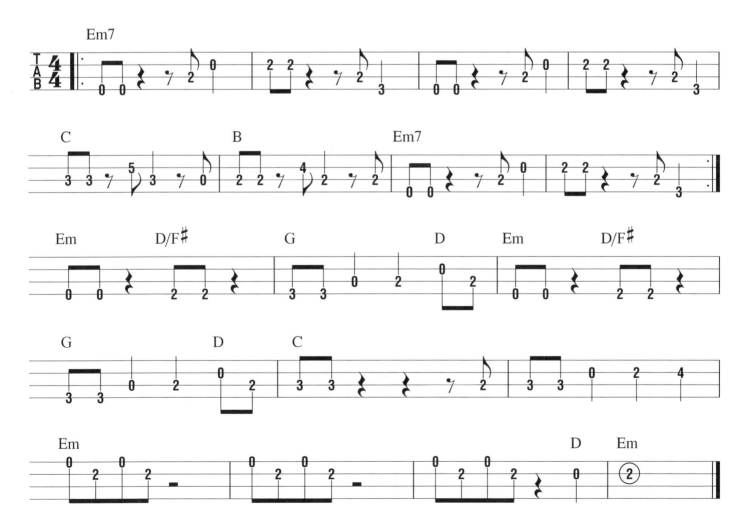

Closing Note

Congratulations on teaching yourself to play the bass guitar! You've hardly reached the end of the line, though. There's much more to learn, so keep practicing your technique, scales, and arpeggios, and continue your studies with other books or possibly a private instructor. Also remember to try and jam with other musicians whenever possible. It's a fun learning experience that will expand your musical horizons. Good luck!